MOTORBIKES

Frances Ridley

Editorial Consultant – Cliff Moon

RISING★STARS

nasen

nasen
NASEN House, 4/5 Amber Business Village, Amber Close,
Amington, Tamworth, Staffordshire B77 4RP

Rising Stars UK Ltd.
22 Grafton Street, London W1S 4EX
www.risingstars-uk.com

Every effort has been made to trace copyright holders and obtain their permission for use of copyright material. The publisher will gladly receive information enabling them to rectify any error or omission in subsequent editions.
All facts are correct at time of going to press.

Text © Rising Stars UK Ltd.
The right of Frances Ridley to be identified as the author of this work has been asserted by her in accordance with the Copyright, Design and Patents Act, 1988.

First published 2006

Cover design: Button plc
Cover image: Alamy
Illustrator: Bill Greenhead
Text design and typesetting: Marmalade Book Design
(www.marmaladebookdesign.com)
Educational consultants: Cliff Moon, Lorraine Petersen and Paul Blum
Technical consultant: Mark Rendes
Pictures: Alamy: pages 6-7, 10, 11, 12, 13, 14, 15, 16, 18, 19, 20, 21, 22, 25, 27, 30, 31, 32-33, 38, 40, 41
Empics: pages 4-5, 9, 15, 42, 42-43, 46
Getty Images: pages 17, 26, 39
National Motoring Museum: 24

British Library Cataloguing in Publication Data.
A CIP record for this book is available from the British Library.

ISBN: 978-1-84680-045-0

Printed by Craftprint International Ltd., Singapore

Contents

Motorbikes

People ride motorbikes for different reasons.

Some people want to ride short distances.
Some people want to ride long distances.
Other people just want to ride fast!

Motorbike design

All motorbikes have the same basic design.

Many bikes also have a fairing. This is the coloured shell that fits over the motorbike's chassis.

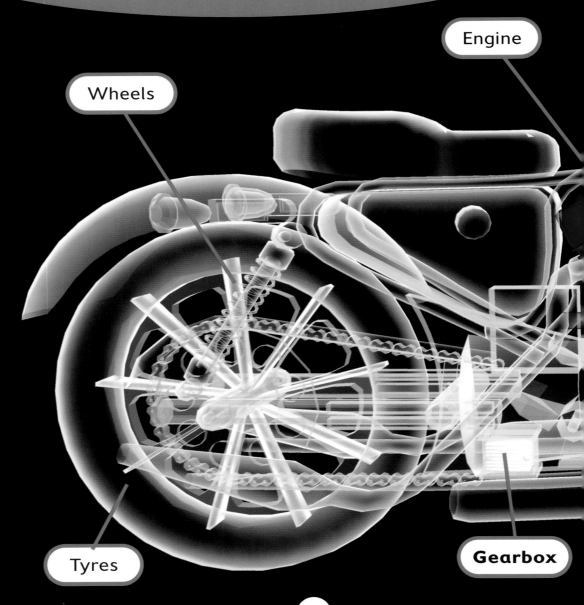

Engine

Wheels

Tyres

Gearbox

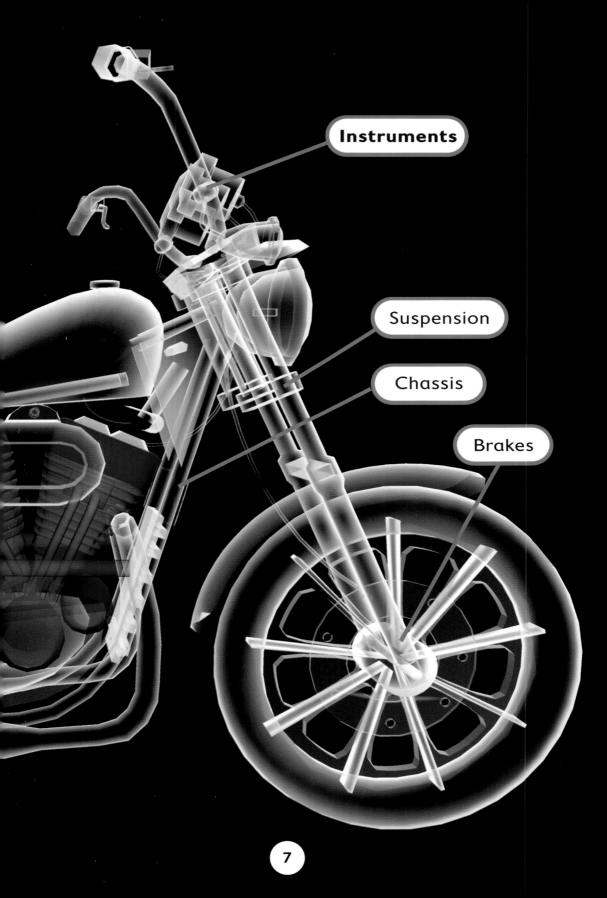

Instruments

Suspension

Chassis

Brakes

Motorbike engines

Types of engine

Most modern motorbikes have four-stroke petrol engines.

1 Suck

Petrol and air sucked in.

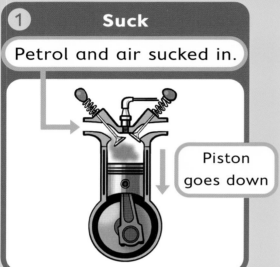

Piston goes down

2 Squeeze

Petrol and air squeezed.

3 Bang

Petrol and air set alight.

4 Blow

Burned gases let out as exhaust.

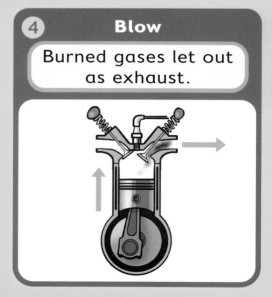

A four-stroke engine **cycle**.

Engine layout

Designers lay out engine cylinders in different ways.

Layout	Diagram
Single	
Parallel twin	
V-twin	
Opposed twin	
In-line four (most common)	

Engine capacity

Engine capacity is measured in cc.

Most learner bikes are 125cc.

Sports bikes go from 400cc to 1300cc engines.

Classic bikes

Brough Superior – 1919 to 1940

Each Brough Superior was **custom-made** for its owner.

This Superior was made for **Lawrence of Arabia**.

George Brough tested each bike himself.

An SS100 had to reach 100 mph.

An SS80 had to reach 80 mph.

Brough raced on his Superiors.

In 1928, Brough recorded 130.6 mph on an SS100, which was a world record!

Vincent Black Shadow – 1948

The Vincent Black Shadow was black all over.

Even its engine and gear box were black.

Its top speed was 122 mph – much faster than any other bike of the time.

Large 150 mph speedometer

American cruisers

America is a big country so American riders want strong, comfortable bikes.

Indian

The Indian Company made
motorcycles from 1901 to 1953.

The Scout was a famous Indian bike.

Low saddle

Long frame

Indian Scout, 1931 model

Indian's slogan was:

'You can't wear out an Indian Scout,
it will wear you out first.'

Harley-Davidson

Harley-Davidson started in 1903 and it still makes bikes today.

It's famous for its low, heavy cruisers.

1936 – 61EL Knucklehead

This is a **classic** Harley-Davidson bike.

Teardrop fuel tank

Curved mudguards

1937 – U Navy

Harley-Davidson made these bikes for the Navy to use in World War II.

Fishtail silencer

Gun holder

1972 – XR750

Evel Knievel used the XR750 for his stunts.

Customised bikes

People didn't have much money after World War II.

They customised their bikes instead of buying new ones.

In America, riders took off bike parts that they didn't want.

They called their customised bikes ' choppers'.

They 'chopped' off mudguards, indicators, the saddle and even the front brakes!

In Europe, riders put the engine from one bike into the frame of another bike.

The riders met at motorway cafés to race the bikes so they called their bikes 'café racers'.

The 1969 film **Easy Rider** is about a motorbike gang.

The gang ride customised Harley-Davidson bikes.

The film started a craze for choppers in the 1970s.

Customising is still popular today.

There are Chopper Conventions in America and Britain.

'American Chopper' is a top TV programme in America.

It is a reality show about customising motorbikes.

Tracks (Part one)

I look out of the shop window. Sam's outside.

"Go on," his mouth says. "Do it!"

My heart's beating loud.

I grab the nearest magazine and stuff it up my top.

Suddenly, a hand grabs my shoulder. I freeze with fear!

This lad is grinning down at me. Gently, he pulls out the magazine.

"So," he says. "You like motorbikes, right?"

I nod – too scared to speak.

He puts his hand in his pocket. He's going to call the police!

But he doesn't pull out his mobile – he pulls out a leaflet.

"Go to Tracks," he says. "You won't regret it. Tell Bill that Jon sent you."

Continued on page 28

Road bikes

Road bikes are called roadsters or commuters. They are fun, all-round bikes and they are cheaper than sports bikes.

Most road bikes are **unfaired**.

The Suzuki Bandit 600S is a popular **half-faired** roadster.

Tourers

Tourers are designed to go on long trips.
The king of tourers is the Honda Goldwing.
The latest Goldwing model is the GL1800.

Raised passenger seat

Space for bags

25-litre fuel tank

Off-road bikes

An off-road bike needs good suspension and tyres with good grip.

The body is high to stop it scraping the ground.

Front suspension

The Yamaha YZ250 is a popular motocross bike.

Motocross bikes race round cross-country tracks with jumps and hills.

The bottom of a motocross bike must be well clear of the ground.

Motocross bikes also need good **acceleration** and good brakes.

Enduro bikes race over long distances.

The most famous Enduro race is the Paris –
Dakar Rally. The motorbikes race in the
desert. They need large fuel tanks to last
in the desert.

The Paris – Dakar Rally.

Mopeds and scooters

Scooters and mopeds are small, light bikes.

They are:

- cheap to buy

- cheap to run – they don't use much petrol

- good in traffic

- easy to ride and park.

Italy has made scooters since World War II.

Factories were banned from making planes after the war. So they made Vespas instead.

Modern Italian scooters.

Mopeds are slower
and less powerful
than scooters.

16-year-olds
can ride mopeds
on the road in
the UK.

Tracks (Part two)

"You didn't nick anything!" says Sam.
"You're useless! Forget about being in my gang!"

"I've got better things to do!" I shout.

But I haven't got better things to do.
I've blown it.

Then I remember the leaflet.

"Why not?" I think.

Tracks is a huge garage. Inside, kids are customising two motorbikes.

A man comes over.

"I'm Bill," he says. "Can I help you?"

"I'm Adam – Jon sent me."

"Right," said Bill. "Put these overalls on."

I spend the rest of the day at Tracks.
It's brilliant! Bill and the other kids show me
what to do with the bikes. I pick it up really
fast – I feel proud of myself!

"Coming next Saturday?" asks Bill.

"You bet!" I tell him.

Continued on page 34

The first superbikes

The first modern superbikes were made by BSA. They were the BSA Rocket 3 and the Triumph T150 Trident.

The two bikes were almost the same.

They were launched in Britain in 1969.

BSA Rocket 3

Tilted engine

	Trident	Rocket
Top speed	122 mph	122 mph
Capacity	740 cc	740 cc
Engine	Three-cylinder	Three-cylinder
Weight	222 kg	219 kg

'Ray gun' silencers

Vertical engine

Triumph T150 Trident

Honda CB750

Honda's CB750 was launched in 1969.

It had:

- a 4-cylinder engine

- **hydraulic disc brakes**

- an **electric starter**.

None of these things was new.

But nobody had put them all into a **production** bike before.

The CB750 was Honda's first big bike – and it was a big hit!

Top speed	124 mph
Capacity	736 cc
Engine	In-line four
Weight	220 kg

Tracks (Part three)

I've been going to Tracks for a month now.

The bikes are looking really good.

Last week, I met Sam.

"You're never around these days," he moaned.

"I'm surprised you noticed," I said. "You must be so busy with your gang."

Then I told him about Tracks and how brilliant it is.

"Maybe I'll come along," he said.

****

It's Saturday, and Sam has come to Tracks!

We work on the bikes all morning and then take a break.

"What do you think?" I ask.

"It's OK," says Sam.

"What about Bill – he's brilliant, isn't he?"

"Not that brilliant," says Sam. "Look what I lifted from him just now."

And he shows me a wallet and grins.

Continued on the next page

After the break, Bill asks the thief to own up.

"You may have to leave Tracks," says Bill. "But if you don't own up I'll have to close Tracks down. We can't run this place if we can't trust each other."

I look at Sam. I don't want to tell on him but I don't want to lose Tracks. Sam goes very red. Suddenly, he pulls out the wallet and hands it to Bill.

"I'm sorry," says Sam. "I'll go now."

"Wait," says Bill. He turns to the rest of us.
"Shall we give Sam a second chance?"

All of us have been in trouble before. All of us
have had a second chance at Tracks.
There's only one right answer …

…"Yes!" we shout back.

Modern superbikes

Ducati 916

The Ducati 916 was sleek and **streamlined**.

It looked good and **handled** well and it was powerful and fast.

Exhaust tucked under the seat

Twin headlights fitted into fairing

The Ducati 916 was the top racing bike of its day.

It won five World Superbike Championships.

Carl Fogarty won three rider's titles on a Ducati 916.

Top speed	166 mph
Capacity	916 cc
Engine	4-stroke V-twin
Weight	195 kg

MV Agusta 4

MV Agusta was a big name in racing from the 1950s to the 1970s.

Then it pulled out of racing. It returned in 1998 with the stunning F4.

Stacked headlights

F4 fact!

Massimo Tamburini designed both the Ducati 916 and the MV Agusta F4.

Exhaust under the seat

MV Agusta's racing bikes are red and silver.

Top speed	168 mph
Capacity	In-line four
Engine	749 cc
Weight	190 kg

Kawasaki Ninja ZX-10R

Kawasaki launched the Ninja ZX-10R in 2005.

It is ultra-narrow, light, powerful and very fast!

Kawasaki racing bikes are lime green.

Top speed	186 mph
Capacity	998 cc
Engine	In-line four
Weight	175 kg

Carl Fogarty

Carl Fogarty was born in England in 1966.

He was a top superbike rider.

His nickname was Foggy.

Fogarty was famous for his cornering.

Carl broke the lap record at the **Isle of Man TT** in 1992. His record wasn't broken again for seven years!

Carl Fogarty stopped racing in 2000.

Now he leads the Foggy Petronas Superbike team.

Quiz

1 What is a fairing?

2 What engine capacity do most learner bikes have?

3 What was the Vincent Black Shadow's top speed?

4 When did Harley-Davidson make the U Navy?

5 How did 'choppers' get their name?

6 Name a famous Enduro race.

7 Which company made the Trident and the Rocket?

8 How many times did the Ducati 916 win the World Superbike Championships?

9 What is Carl Fogarty's nickname?

10 What colour are Kawasaki racing bikes?

Glossary of terms

acceleration A change in speed.

classic Does not date – a classic bike still looks good today.

custom-made Made to suit the owner.

cycle One full time round.

electric starter A way of starting the engine.

engine capacity The total internal size of an engine's cylinders.

half-faired With half a fairing.

handling How easy the bike is to ride. A bike handles well if it is easy to steer and brake.

hydraulic disc brakes Metal discs fixed to the wheels which are gripped by a hydraulically-operated brake system.

instruments Give information about speed, distance and revs per minute – not many bikes have a fuel gauge.

Isle of Man TT A road race round the Isle of Man.

Lawrence of Arabia A great British war hero.

production Made to sell to people.

streamlined A smooth shape that lets the air flow over an object. Streamlining the shape of a bike may help it to go much faster.

unfaired Without fairing.

More resources

Books

Hugo Wilson's Hot Bikes by Hugo Wilson
Published by Dorling Kindersley
ISBN: 0-7513-3694-7
Pictures and information on 300 great bikes.

Superbikes (Designed for Success Series) by Ian Graham
Published by Heinemann Library
ISBN: 0431165718
Find out how the world's top superbikes are designed and made.

Magazines

Bike Magazine
The best-selling motorbike magazine in Britain – it covers all types of bike.

DVDs

Chopper Kings (2005)
Duke Marketing Ltd. (Cat. No. B00092ZE0U)
Take a trip across America to find out more about customising bikes.

World Superbike Reviews (2005)
Duke Marketing Ltd. (Cat. No. B000BAZDF6)
Duke make a review of the WSB Championship every year. Check out races and riders!

Websites

Try the BBC for motorbike news at this address:
http://news.bbc.co.uk/sport1/hi/motorsport/motorbikes/default.stm

The BBC also has information on riding and buying bikes.
http://www.bbc.co.uk/motoring/twowheels/index.shtml

This website has an online gallery of motorbike pictures.
http://www.motosites.com/Motorcycle_Gallery/

Answers

1 The shell that fits over a motorbike's chassis.

2 125cc

3 122 mph

4 During World War II.

5 Riders 'chopped' bits off their bikes to customise them.

6 The Paris-Dakar Rally.

7 BSA

8 3

9 Foggy

10 Lime green

Index